TO

_____

_____

_____

FROM

_____

MY SISTER, MY FRIEND

Published by in 2012 Struik Inspirational Gifts
New Holland Publishing (South Africa) (Pty) Ltd
(New Holland Publishing is a member of Avusa Ltd)
First Floor, Wembley Square
Solan Street, Gardens
Cape Town 8001

Reg. No. 1971/009721/07

Project management and selection by Reinata Thirion
DTP by Monique Botma
Cover design by Monique Botma
Images from Shutterstock
Printed and bound in Singapore

ISBN 978-1-4153-2122-5

www.struikinspirationalgifts.co.za

STRUIK INSPIRATIONAL GIFTS

MY SISTER,
my friend

Brothers and *sisters* are as close as *hands* and feet.

— VIETNAMESE PROVERB

Loneliness is the *first* thing which God's eye named not *good*.

— AUTHOR UNKNOWN

Are we *not* like
two volumes of
one book?

– Marceline Desbordes-Valmore

The best thing *about* having a sister was that I always had a *friend*.

– CALI RAE TURNER

In the *cookies* of life, sisters are the *chocolate* chips.

A *sister* shares childhood memories and grown-up *dreams*.

— ANONYMOUS

Having a *sister* is like having a *best friend* you can't get rid of. You know whatever you *do*, they'll still be *there*.

— AMY LI

Shared joy
is a double joy;
shared *sorrow*
is half a sorrow.

— Swedish Proverb

In thee my *soul* shall own
combined the *sister*
and the friend.

— CATHERINE KILLIGREW

A *sister*
is a forever
friend.

– AUTHOR UNKNOWN

Our *roots*
say we're sisters,
our *hearts* say
we're friends.

– AUTHOR UNKNOWN

While we were *born* sisters,
we grew up to
be *friends*.

— CATHERINE PULSIFER

A best *friend*
is a sister destiny
forgot to
give you.

– AUTHOR UNKNOWN

Best friends by *heart*; sisters by *soul*.

— AUTHOR UNKNOWN

A *true* sister
is a **friend** who
listens with
her **heart.**

— Anonymous

A sister is a *gift* to the **heart**, a friend to the spirit, a golden *thread* to the meaning of life.

— ISADORA JAMES

Sisters
are different
flowers from
the same garden.

– AUTHOR UNKNOWN

What's the **good** of *news* if you haven't a *sister* to **share** it?

— Jenny DeVries

A sister can be *seen* as someone who is both ourselves and very much ***not*** ourselves – a special kind of *double*.

— TONI MORRISON

Help one *another*, is **part** of the religion of *sisterhood*.

— LOUISA MAY ALCOTT

God often speaks
to us *through*
a sister's love.

— AUTHOR UNKNOWN

Sweet is the voice
of a *sister* in the
season of sorrow.

— Benjamin Disraeli

Remember, we all stumble, **every** one of us. That's why it's a **comfort** to go *hand* in hand.

— EMILY KIMBROUGH

To have a *loving* relationship with a sister is not *simply* to have a **buddy** or a **confident** – it is to have a *soulmate* for life.

— VICTORIA SECUNDA

With *all* life's treasures and blessings without end, I *have* the finest sister and even *dearer* friend.

— AUTHOR UNKNOWN

When *sisters*
stand shoulder to
shoulder, who ***stands***
a chance against us?

— PAM BROWN

Is *solace* anywhere
more **comforting**
than in the arms
of a sister.

– ALICE WALKER

In the *coldest* winter month, as in every other month in every other year, vthe *best* thing to hold on to in this world is *each* other.

— LINDA ELLERBEE

You *know* the song in my **heart** and *sing* it to me when my **memory** *fails*.

— DONNA ROBERTS

If fame were based on *kindness* instead of **popularity**, on understanding and *not* on worldwide **attention**, you **would be** the biggest celebrity on *earth*.

— Anonymous

We would like to hear from you.
Please send your comments about this book to us at:
reviews@struikinspirationalgifts.co.za

For exciting new releases and to buy online,
visit www.struikchristianmedia.co.za

STRUIK INSPIRATIONAL GIFTS

BEAUTY. PASSION. INSPIRATION.

www.struikinspirationalgifts.co.za